Dungheap Cockerel

low treasons
incited by
Rip Bulkeley

and abetted by
Culture Matters

First published 2023 by **Culture Matters**.
Culture Matters Co-Operative Ltd. promotes a socialist and progressive
approach to art, culture and politics. See www.culturematters.org.uk

Text copyright © the contributors
Front & Back Cover & Illustrations © Mike Dicks and Martin Gollan
Edited by Rip Bulkeley
Layout and typesetting by Alan Morrison
ISBN: 978-1-912710-62-1

Contents

Pictures

The illustrations by Mike Dicks and Martin Gollan were kindly provided by their authors at the editor's request.

The etching of the Peterloo Massacre is in the public domain and was downloaded from Wikimedia Commons.

Introduction

By Rip Bulkeley and Mike Quille

Hundreds of millions of pounds were spent on the coronation in an effort to rally national sentiment behind King Charles. This extravagant celebration of unearned wealth took place amid a cost-of-capitalism crisis that is forcing full-time workers to resort to foodbanks to feed their kids, while the corporate crooks running our country into the ground post record profits.

Attempts to enrol His Majesty's subjects in a spontaneous display of subjugation, through urging them to declaim oaths of allegiance from their sitting rooms, met such a limp response that the Palace has leaked disclaimers suggesting the King was never a fan of the idea.

Polls suggest support for the monarchy is at an all-time low, especially among the young. But why should socialists stir up the hornets' nest of republicanism, when the monarchy is of limited relevance to most people's lives and was personified until recently by a widely liked queen of many decades' standing?

That queen is now dead, though, and there are ominous signs that the coronation of Charles III is not harmless spectacle. The monarchy is the pinnacle of the British state and that state's increasing authoritarianism has been on full display since Charles came to the throne. Police swooped on peaceful protesters at events proclaiming him king in several British cities. Some were arrested simply for holding up blank pieces of paper. Royal assent has just been given to the Public Order Act, the latest in a long line of repressive laws passed since the 2019 election.

Police now have sweeping powers to shut down protest, and the Met—unfazed by its own reputation lying in tatters because of racism, misogyny and homophobia—has warned it intends to use them. Its threat to crack down on 'anyone intent on undermining' the coronation is chilling. The police will give their new powers the widest interpretation possible. With the Tories, their aim is a new normal in which people will think twice before protesting in public because of the risks.

The thuggish intimidation of republicans is inseparable from the project to shrink the range of permissible political opinion after the shock the Corbyn surge gave the ruling class—something policed most ferociously by the Labour Party, which has itself made a meal of exaggerated royalism since Keir Starmer took over. The character-assassination campaign against Corbyn himself regularly involved allegations of disrespect towards the monarchy—and the monarchy's place above Parliament was cited by generals briefing the press that the army might have to remove an elected socialist government. Nor should it be forgotten that the monarchy, greedily supported by a sycophantic aristocracy, is the main foundation of the inegalitarian and corrupt system of land ownership in Britain, an outrage that is centuries overdue for reform.

So the monarchy is not neutral. It can appear so when the status quo is not threatened, but its undemocratic state power will be deployed if the ruling class consider it necessary to prevent radical change—as it was in Australia in 1975 with the removal of socialist prime minister Gough Whitlam. And the growing opposition to monarchy should not be separated from wider political trends either. It is bound up with anger at an unrepresentative and oppressive British state and an economy rigged against ordinary people.

The popularity of the monarchy among a large swathe of the British public is sad evidence of their infantilization and the extent to which they have internalized the tropes of the most entrenched and wicked class system the world has known since the fall of Rome.

The army of rough sleepers that colonizes London today, the survivors of Grenfell, the 14 million living in poverty in Britain, all those who have found themselves on the receiving end of a battering in the name of austerity this past decade, including the loved ones of the 120,000 who have died as a direct result, are entitled to ask when the revolution will begin.

Protest against the coronation is justified. Socialists should work to build it into a movement for democracy that challenges more than just the monarchy, that demands not merely economic and political, but also constitutional and cultural change in Britain. For the time has surely come to sweep away the gown and wig of semi-feudalism that underpins our major institutions—the Commons, House of Lords, judiciary and, yes, the monarchy.

The poets and cartoonists in these pages are prophets of that transformative change. While the poets denounce first the institution, then its current incumbent, and finally his obsolete initiation rigmarole, cartoonist Martin Gollan underlines many of their twists and turns. Meanwhile the laid-back Brighton parodist Mike Dicks intervenes to poke fun at the dysfunctional Windsors and to mock the British weather, which on 6 May 2023 offered its own comment on the notoriously damp monarch. Needless to say we are grateful to all those who offered us their contributions. Lastly, the lesson of the American Revolution bears repeating some 250 years later: not even the most capitalist of dungheaps has any need whatsoever for a cockerel.

The existence of a hereditary monarchy helps to prop up all the privilege and patronage that corrupts our society; that is why the crown is seen as being of such importance to those who run the country—or enjoy the privileges it affords.

—Tony Benn

Humanity will never be free until the last king is strangled with the entrails of the last priest.

—Denis Diderot

The Peterloo Massacre

'To Henry Hunt, Esq., as chairman of the meeting assembled in St. Peter's Field, Manchester, sixteenth day of August, 1819, and to the female Reformers of Manchester and the adjacent towns who were exposed to and suffered from the wanton and fiendish attack made on them by that brutal armed force, the Manchester and Cheshire Yeomanry Cavalry, this plate is dedicated by their fellow labourer, Richard Carlile.'

* Carlile was sentenced to six years in Dorchester Gaol after he published this etching and an account of "The Manchester Massacre" in his newspaper *The Republican*.

England in 1819

An old, mad, blind, despised, and dying King;
Princes, the dregs of their dull race, who flow
Through public scorn,—mud from a muddy spring;
Rulers who neither see nor feel nor know,
But leechlike to their fainting country cling
Till they drop, blind in blood, without a blow.
A people starved and stabbed in th' untilled field;
An army, whom liberticide and prey
Makes as a two-edged sword to all who wield;
Golden and sanguine laws which tempt and slay;
Religion Christless, Godless—a book sealed;
A senate, Time's worst statute, unrepealed—
Are graves from which a glorious Phantom may
Burst, to illumine our tempestuous day.

Percy Bysshe Shelley

Some Things That Go Before King, Martin Gollan

Some Things That Go Before King

counterchec, rubbernec
strikebrea, pissta,
heartbrea, troublema
multitas, unmas
bluestoc, foreloc
motherfuc, bloodsuc
wisecrac, backtrac
benchmar, disembar
pawnbro, keystro
stockbro, anti-smo,
undercoo, overloo
hyperlin, freethin
hallmar, reembar
hitchhi, motorbi
bootlic, politic
rollic, nitpic
lovema, muckra

ransac, carjac,

miskic, picnic
upchuc, untuc
knoc, cloc, floc, doc
pric, tric, snac, smac
strea, spea, cor, for
lur, jer, har, bar
kin, lin, sin, win
hac, jac, jo, po
nu, pu, suc, fuc
ran, tan, yan, wan
stri, vi, bi, hi, li, pi
not my

Janine Booth

Off With Their Heads

The dance of death
The gallows length

Who holds the rope
That hangs the head

Who framed the damned
Who met the axe

Who condemns the body
To the autopsist's stash

Who wiped a country
Off the map

Who turned many a man
To a pillar of ash

Who is the one
Behind the mask

The nation state
The bloody hand

Johnny Giles

Application for the Role of Queen

Some little girls dream of being princesses. Many of you may be unaware that before taking up the role of Queen Consort, Camilla had always wanted to be a queen, and this wasn't the first time she tried to fill in an application form.

I have gained access to an earlier attempt and wish to share it with you.

Please complete this cover sheet before attempting the rest of the form.

Please answer YES or NO to the following:

1: Are you prepared to have an alter-ego called Dave who has a boring job in accounts?

NO

2. Are you prepared to carry your own regalia in a battered suitcase?

NO

3. Are you prepared to travel and stop at Premier Inns when appropriate?

NO

4. Are you prepared to travel by Jumbo bus?

NO

5. Are you prepared to complete your makeup in less than two hours?

NO

6. Are you prepared, or do you already know, all the lyrics in Kylie Minogue's back catalogue?

NO

7. Are you prepared to do the splits?

NO

8. Are you prepared to use gaffer tape in your intimate area?

NO

9. Are you prepared to slut drop at a moment's notice?

NO

10. Are you prepared to be laughed at?

NO

11. Are you prepared to be heckled, ridiculed, spat at, disowned and generally treated like shit?

NO

12. Are you prepared to walk with your head held high in 6 inch heels?

NO

If you have answered YES to all of the above then you may be just the queen we are looking for. So please apply.

Thank you for your interest in our company.

We are proud to be an equal opportunities employer.

(Of course this time Camilla didn't have to apply. She knew someone who knew someone who was related to someone, so she got the job.)

Anne Babbs

The King Is Mad

The king is mad.
The queen bears his children
like a malady.
It would be a simple solution,

were she to eat them before
they grow into their own madness.
She does not. She lets them
scamper about, small birds

that twitter and fret
in every corner of the palace.
The king is growing a beard
to cover his own curse,

it trails behind him
like a grey rag.
He is losing shape
in his own emptiness.

Yet, in this contagion
he is also grown more still,
rising from his beard and robes
like a statue of himself

raised to himself.
There is something to be said
for such a quiet madness.
Perhaps we envy him.

Philip Kane

On The Day the Queen Died   *

I wondered about a Roman urn
on display in a Welsh country house.
Whose ashes had it contained,
what remnants of black dust are these
that still cling to the inner surface?

Jagged fractures pattern the outside,
broken pieces of clay glued together
like some coarse kintsugi,
but the pot seems almost whole again
and carries its mystery with a simple dignity.

Were the ashes of a now nameless foreign leader
held within and buried here in this Welsh soil,
were those residues taken up
by the roots of grasses and trees
of this open green parkland place?

All that is left now of the remains of a life
is a kind of silence, an unknowing.
Those who mourned are also long gone
but yet, we still consider, who was it,
how did they live, how did they die?

Were they a revered hero? A heroine?
And in another 2000 years who will wonder about her,
that majestic one who died today?
She'll be buried in a lead-lined coffin,
her name engraved forever.

Yet in the year 4022
as people stand before her long-cold tomb
what will she mean to them?

Jackie Biggs

* *Newton House, NT Dinefwr, 8 September 2022. On display, a Roman urn found in the
remains of a Roman fort in what is now Dinefwr Parkland, probably C100-200AD, thought
to contain a cremation.*

6

I Saw Prince Andrew in Pizza Express

I saw Prince Andrew in Pizza Express
at the Metro Centre in Gateshead.
He had the Pollo Forza, with an extra topping
of Kobe beef and oysters,
and a side order of foie gras
lightly dusted in saffron,
washed down with a bottle of Château d'Yquem,
and for dessert,
truffles rolled in the finest Italian chocolate.
By the time he'd finished he was
sweating profusely.
The waiter said it was on the house,
on account of all he does for the country.

I saw Prince Andrew in Pizza Express
at Trinity Walk in Wakefield.
He had the Barbacoa, with an extra topping
of wealth accrued by exploiting the peasantry,
and a side order of 10%
of the county's annual produce,
washed down with the tears of the widows of
                    soldiers killed in the hundred years' war,
and for dessert,
the Droit de Seigneur.
By the time he'd finished he was
loudly proclaiming his family's divine right to rule.
The waiter said it was on the house,
and something unspecific about tourism.

I saw Prince Andrew in Pizza Express
at Teesside Park in Stockton.
He had the Sloppy Giuseppe, with an extra topping
of plunder from Africa and the Indian subcontinent,
and a side order of confiscated gold
from the dissolution of the monasteries,

washed down with the blood of rebels executed
                        during the Mau Mau Uprising,
and for dessert,
strawberry ice cream.
By the time he'd finished he was
arguing the unfairness of judging the current
                        ruling class by the actions of its predecessors.
The waitress charged him double.
I think she was Argentinian.

I don't like Prince Andrew, or Pizza Express.
I very rarely go there.
That's why I remember it all
so distinctly.

Joe Williams

Buckingham Shed

Some children have imaginary friends.
I had a shed, a gate and a map
which led to an unexplored garden
a polo stroke away
from a big overgrown house.
If I peeked through
the shed's weathered boards
I could turn this big house
into a big palace
turn the east wing into an aviary
the west wing
into a museum of scarecrows
fly flags of robins in the parks
and the fields of the countryside
which I'd pass through
until my pocket money ran out
and I'd be back in my shed
growing magically-modified turnips
and thinking about the train
leaving platform eleven
from my imaginary railway station in life.
I carried my garden shed to school
and out on my newspaper round.
I smuggled it
on the bus to town
and smuggled it back.
I took it to see
Lady Chatterley's Lover at the Gaumont
and stood with it at the end
when they played the National Anthem.
Back in Wild West Park
I took it out
with my imaginary pack of feral cats
and hunted imaginary corgis.
I was born in November

two days after Halloween.
The day I started secondary school
my mother sent me the keys
to Buckingham Shed
and a kingdom of weeds
while my father gave me
an exercise book
and a Mickey Mouse pen
with which I wrote Christmas speeches
from the monarchy in the shadows.
When I was small
I'd sing pop songs all over utopia
and I'd be rich and famous
and meet Alan Freeman,
David Jacobs and Cathy McGowan.
My first rock and roll band
were called The Buckingham Shed Collective.
They were always top of the bill
and talk of the allotment.
In Buckingham Shed
I was taller than any tree
I ever climbed in Woodland Wood.
In my shed I'd flick through
wildlife shots of wise old owls
and read *Trout Fishing on Treasure Island*
as they filled their larders with field mice.
Sometimes the owls would discuss
critical theory with a flock of crows
under an imaginary sky
under which Ted Hughes was standing
the last in a long line
of collected Poet Laureates
each one wearing a poetry medal
for services to the imagination.

Kenny Knight

Ruling From the Tomb

The tradition of the dead generations weighs like a
nightmare on the minds of the living.
                                        —Karl Marx

Let the drums beat out a dirge.
Paint the epitaphs on every wall.
Things change to remain the same.
Dip the flags, but don't let them fall.
The people can dance late into the night
As long as keep they within their limits.
Those born to hold the golden hour
Can spare one or two precious minutes.
They work hard who protect and serve
Just to keep a lid on a boiling pot.
Occasionally pouring out a ladle or two
To those who could easily have the lot.
Some say it is all so unfair
But things won't be any different soon
While the traditions of the dead generations
Are still ruling from the tomb.

Phil Knight

RIP the Queue, Martin Gollan

RIP The Queue

Your final day on this planet
13 hours long at times
Films were made of you
Celebrities cheated on you
You could be seen from space
But no one could save a space
5 miles long you were
A strange phenomenon
That entered the Guinness book of records
Oh queue, how fondly you will be remembered
How we laughed at you
So many solemn faces outside
Temporary heartbreaking inside
Queue, queue, queue
What will we do now you have gone
Now that the box that was at the end has gone
Will you not stay and say you need to see the space the box has vacated
Be a permanent marker in our lives
The queue
Gone but not forgotten

Fin Hall

No More Old King and Country

No more old King and Country
It's more like humpty dumpty

Or the Grand Old Duke of Scrumpy
Serving humbly serving numbly

The casualties are apple seeds
The kind of fruit one shouldn't eat

No matter how juicy the 'Glory'
No-one needs an end that's gory

Forget all the ancient stories
Take them as dark allegories

Johnny Giles

God Save Us

God save us from the queen
Gross pomp and wealth obscene
    Greedy and mean.
A ten-million pound *coach of gold?*
While people freeze in the cold?
Poverty stalks young and old
    Who needs a queen?

Let this queen be our last
In dustbins of the past
Dump all her lousy class
    Set ourselves free!
Time for flags to be furled
We only have one world
    and it must be free!

Why celebrate a tic?
This whole thing makes me sick
    Ych a fi—Royalty!
No other parasite
Cockroach housefly or mite
Tapeworms, pond-leeches, fleas—
They don't get jubilees
    Why then a queen?

Greed should be a disgrace.
Send them to outer space
(or a much better place)
God save the Human Race
    All equally!

We don't need the
Self-serving parasite
Bastion of the Right
It's gonna be a fight
but we must be free!

Tear flags and borders down
No need for kids to drown
Plenty to go around
    If we were free
Workers do everything
We don't need queen, boss or king
    We must be free!

P.S. (May '23) That wasn't quite what I meant
(queen to be heaven-sent)
    (But thanks anyway.)

This song has sure done its thing
We're now lumbered with a king
    We're only halfway!
Coated in stolen bling—
Still not worth a thing
Still can't do anything
    Take him away!

No need to re-write this song
Only the rhyme is wrong
All else here still applies
We are up to our eyes
    Royalty?
    Ych a fi!

Heather Booker

St Edward's Crown

Remove the jewels
And melt the crown
Bury the old way
Under the ground

We have no need for
A blowhard's bling
Down with the detestable
Rule of Kings

Sling your hook
And all your rings
Like Robin Hood
Or Dick Turpin

The ignoble Noble
Pretend they hath no sin
Who rules is who wins
They whinge

Johnny Giles

Spot-on Room 101

for your time has come, my friends,
I'd like to see you gone for good.
So (as everyone these days must say
before they start), here's my choice:

the common cold, I'm sick of you,
the blocked and bleeding nose, the cough—
I want to see you off, and can't believe
that anyone will disagree with me;

next, pontificating politicians playing games
with other people's lives, calling names, and simply
(I'll try to be polite) adding gloss to their untruths
to make us fools again to take them at their word,
and if we can't persuade them to get lost, at least
a massive fine for every lie they tell or, better still,
the 'opportunity' to live among the rest of us in
this lovely boat they've helped create;

and lastly, though resistance will be tough,
all weapons that make use of metal,
as bows and arrows will give non-human
animals as well as us a bit more luck.

Oh yes, and while I'm here, top one, a bonus choice,
I'd like to dump the monarchy and all their hangers on,
and if there is no room in 101 to fit them in, a better
perfect chance: just pack them off to where they have
pre-loved facilities to deal with them—in France.

Denni Turp

Uncrooned Kings an Queens Aw Roon

Ah jist popped in when passin by
Tae gie yersel, Oor Rab, ma ee,
The day when no yin man's a king.
Mon oot a dauner, scrieve an sing
An tell the world again jist hoo
A man's a man, for aye, for noo,
For lang as men an weemin ken
Yon croon's for yin heid, no for them
Whae'll never weer it—oor ain croon
Is whit's abuin, ablo, aw roon.

Stuart Paterson

Uncrowned Kings and Queens All Around

I just popped in when passing by
To give yourself, Our Robert, my eye,
Today when no one man's a king.
Come out for a walk, write and sing
And tell the world again just how
A man's a man, always, now,
For as long as men and women know
That crown's for one head, not for them
Who will never wear it—our own crown
Is what's above, below, all around.

19

Our Mountains, Atlasing the World, Martin Gollan

Our Mountains, Atlasing the World

our shoulders born for bearing,
       elevating, from weird guttural places,
       alofting for their graceless glory
Puck, the goatish king, finds his peoples sweet terrain for
       climbing the crags of our nodding heads,
       on snagging necks, and fresh cut hair
the ridges of our bodies used in ungainly purchase
       to better sneer the softness of our parching skin
       to louder cheer the fusing wire of their kin's fur

thoughtfully they chew the straw
       of our jaunting bonnets,
       reverbing the haunt of hymnals
       to horns and to gravy

their hooving smears our make up
       as they deign to climb,
       jeering their bucking joy
they mock us the destiny we choose
       of forever wearing hoof prints
       in our beards, on our faces, in our fresh cut hair
bleating wild, kidding curses
       forbidding tones pitching down
       the anthem's closing verses
remade even as the cooks among us
       prepare the sharpened sticks anew
       slow circulate wise recipes for spicy, curried, stew

Jim Jepps

Screw the King

I am not a subject
I am a topic
I am a simile
I am a facsimile
I am an oblique understatement
Understatement is oblique. It arrives unexpectedly,
glancing off the unobserved side of things.
As Jane once said 'Understatement provides you with
less so you feel more'.
But they want you to be less.
And I feel more distant from the alternate reality
where swearing allegiance to an imaginary,
caring human,
with untold riches
and condescending tone, is the norm.
Yet the media won't leave us alone.
Urging us to be good chanting citizens
to someone, who in another world
could be a dictator.
and later, when he's gone
his subsequent son will expect the same gratuitous
forelock tugging, obsequious grovelling
and knowing their place.
For tradition, because they'd have us believe it is
sedition to shout obscenities at
rather than swear to.
They haven't got a clue.
Do you?
He doesn't even deserve to have his title capitalized.
Are you surprised I feel like that?

You can stick your coronation
It's not my effing nation
You can stick your coronation
Up your arse

Fin Hall

The King's Speech

Not long ago we thought and read
and through communion with the dead
our mind's eye taught us through the night,
measured our feet and cued their flight.
From tolerance to the royal wave,
literature helped us spot a knave
(the Harrys, laughing at life's game)
—coolly chaotic, bold but tame.

Contemplated or in debate,
the writing on the wall's our fate
arches with every word I write
to the third act of a tyrant type—
beyond the red horizon see
a sickled shape makes wing to thee.

It scours the rooftops overhead,
hovers at windows by your bed,
and spreads its poison through the realm
uprooting ancient oak and elm
with twists, insidious and malign.
All seems to naturally decline.
Trustafarians shed your ethnic throws,
your beads, the trinkets in your nose.

Since you've met yourself in an ancient land
and shaken that ass on foreign sand,
you now may credibly confess
just why you love your country best—
do not let the press intimidate,
or unwoke arguments frustrate.
Are they your voice? Do they speak for you?
Who hired them to run your schools?

Diana teased them for their hate
with her raunchy cards from the deep state
but did she try to crush our pride,
our crown (envied the whole world wide);
or say, 'Put a Blairite on the throne,
some grinning spineless PR drone'?

Oh you English, your trust was cheaply bought,
and your House of Lords was sold for naught
but some flag-waving and a fruit compote.
Young blood now guilds the Russian rot
so that the Queen and churchyard yew
might stand with Putin in the food queue.

History must not repeat itself
so down this vodka (to your health)
with spritzer-sipping socialites,
fireworks like napalm through the night!
The press suppress the common voice,
leaving the masses with no choice

but to hail some angry orator,
some blunted tool, little Hitler.
Za nas! Express your prejudice,
say anything at all—you wish!
Let us all be as honest as we can
to understand the things we ban.

And here's to Diana from her number one fan
—she always was the bigger man.

Deborah Cox

* *'Za nas!'* = *'Cheers!' in Russian, but here it also has overtones of 'After us', as in Louis XV's 'Après nous le déluge'.*

24

Red White and Blue

When I drive past an elder in full flower
on June roads, on some national holiday,
I yearn for its distinctive scent and colour.
There was a poet who saw cow parsley

not as a weed, but a luxuriant
drift of pure colour, white as you need to get.
The wayside swarms with life, red is a field of
poppies, and blue is vivid alkanet.

Tatty bunting obscures the war memorial,
and by the road signs, grass has overgrown.
I look elsewhere—these flags do not concern me—
prefer frail flora and enduring stone.

Merryn Williams

Lament, 6 May 2023, Martin Gollan

Lament, 6 May 2023

It's a realm I no longer recognize.
High-minded regard for profit-based safety
has made a wasteland of the testing ground
for sociability where I learned the game
beside a booming forge. Urban renewal's
dubbed the working men's club a heritage site.
And the crowning glory, the monument
to Aphrodite, where the young nubiles
conferred tongueless kisses in sheltered light
has gone the way of all flesh, leaving only
the sour smell of fuck all. Nearby Little Moscow
where they voted Red out of habit and hope
chiefly betrayed is now Little Warsaw for real.
The council calls it a zone in transition.
You could try living here if you've got talent.
Shop around for charity or place your bets
on the royal colours. Wave a tatty flag
to celebrate tradition, don't lose the plot,
you're on the edge of the periphery,
pissed on, of a country that's so possessed
a wedding pic of a banged-up journalist
would jeopardize national security.

Edward Mackinnon

Anachronism

All you have is the weight of wombs,
the whimpers of women breeding names
to be carved by blood on stone, the reek
of ambition. You carry a cargo of power
and misery, ghostly imprint of madness,
a grand arc of ceremony anointed in holy oils.
You have your flags, your abbeys, your palaces,
your medals, your golden coach, the arrogance
to take your feudal dues. Finger your prizes
behind high walls, wrap secrets in ermine and velvet,
accept the reverence of strangers in payment
for the coincidence of your birth.
All you have is a name, a divine right taken
by a single seed, the clipped wings of ravens.

Liz McPherson

Teabreak

In the supermarket canteen
everything is red, white and blue
except for my grungy purse
and a black pen
in my shirt pocket.

You've been sitting on that chair
since Nineteen Fifty Two.
I must have been
somewhere between crawling and walking
not yet living in Honicknowle
when they gave you that crown
all those palaces and castles
no semi-detached suburbia
no bungalow
no tower block for you.

You waved to me
in the warehouse
on Thursday afternoon
you waved to the crowds
in the patriotic car park
and here I am
in the supermarket canteen
a republican at teabreak
with a handful of raspberries
and a Union Jack serviette.

You've never made it
down to Buckingham Shed
but if you do
bring a tin can for the scarecrow
bring a corgi and a telegram for Lulu.

You're minutes away from being
the same astrological sign
as Melisande and my mum
born on the cusp
of Taurus and Aries.
You've been an old-age pensioner
for thirty years
now you've the same age as Joe 90.
Ninety red, white and blue
candles on a cake.
Ninety tins of dog food
from Lidl and Aldi.

Kenny Knight

The King of I Am 2020

Don't you know who I am?
I'm the King of All I am
Well known by those who need to know
I'm the King of the Great I am

Once caught the reflection of
Deflected sunlight from the
Knowing imperceptible nod of a
Royal who shall be nameless
Lest I betray a confidence
Profound and respected
In certain circles
Placed a call in advance
To secure a table out of sight
In a restaurant I trust
Silver serving
Discretion and integrity
Generously tipped
I'm the King of the Great I am

Badges of honour and
Symbols of office
Confidante and intimate
Storied but never to divulge
I'm the King of the Great I am

The responsibilities of state
Weigh heavy upon my brow
And the press would love to know
The secrets I know now
Such is the life I must endure
Without complaint
As the King of the Great I am

And when the call comes
My duty to discharge
As come the call it must
Then I shall rise to take
My rightful place
As the King of the Great I am

I shall require of course
Your diligence and integrity
In matters of this gravity
For captains of my state
Loyalty will be rewarded
With the ornaments of office
Befitting my indulgence
As the King of the Great I am

Temporarily incognito for now
The King of the Great I am
No pictures please
I'm the King of the Great I am
Strictly need to know
The King of All I am

Ed Tapper

Traitors

I don't want this anthem; he doesn't need saving.
I want one for the homeless, who sleep in the street
these are our boys that did all our killing,
while we installed spikes where they try to sleep.

He begs for food, we blindly walk by him
let them lie on the steps of a bank as it's safe
avoiding the hostel too violent for veterans,
it's safer to die where the money is made.

A quarter of the soldiers in quarters are children
they come back broken, sleep rough in the cold.
Some dream of Empire, these boys are forgotten,
waving our flags, we should be building them homes.

Wear a Poppy on Remembrance Sunday,
but remember these boys we choose to betray.

Patrick Druggan

The Good Old Cause Revived

It is also affirm'd from diligent search made in our ancient books of Law, that the Peers and Barons of England had a legal right to judge the King: which was the cause most likely, for it could be no slight cause, that they were call'd his Peers, or equals. This however may stand immovable, so long as man hath to deal with no better than man; that if our Law judge all men to the lowest by their Peers, it should in all equity ascend also, and judge the highest.

—John Milton, *The Tenure of Kings and Magistrates*, 1649

I tell you, Sirs: I'll bless the day
This new pretender died,
Although I know the price I'll pay,
A signed-up regicide!

Let fortune treat me as it may
Should ill events betide,
Crowned heads regain their ancient sway,
And freedom be denied.

It's Milton's role, the one I'll play,
That poet who supplied
An epic fit to join the fray
With Satan as our guide!

Read it aright and see him stray
From all that's certified
As holy writ and have us weigh
The devil's case clear-eyed.

Then you'll, like me, elect to lay
Old pieties aside,
Think God the devil, and hurray
The rebels in their pride!

It's sovereign power they'd keep at bay,
Demand what's bona fide
About God's role as prop and stay
Of kings with much to hide.

Why keep the wastrels making hay,
Why grant them that free ride,
When there's a quick and ready way
That's all too rarely tried?

I say it's not a man they slay,
Those few who can't abide
The servile thought of mortal clay
By mortal souls enskied.

Divine Right! that's the doctrine they
Revile and one that I'd
Kill in him sooner than betray
The path we've plied.

For there's no king can say us nay,
No future Charles to chide
Us free-born souls who'll not obey
What vassals take in stride.

There's times to come when folk will say
'It's they who stopped the slide;
Else we'd have Charleses to this day,
As Milton prophesied.'

Chris Norris

The King in Ower Town, Martin Gollan

The King in Ower Town

Ee spoke t me
like ee wuz ordinree,
ee .... me? ....
Spoke .... I couldn bleeve,
Im .... King Charles Three
sayz 'Hello!'
like I woz somebuddy
an I'm on'y ....
an ee's so ....
I wuz totelee gobsmacked
I wuz jest wavin
my little Ewnion Jack
an one of an undred
'You don't need to bow!'
'Your Maj ....' ee moved away,
in ower small town
im .... yer .... in-a presink
walkin by-a charitee shops
up t the Red'ouse,
now I feel really important
well, for a moment —
I adto go back
t my blydi freezin flat
with fuckall t eat —
buh f a few seconds
felt like a celebritee,
me .... im .... royalty —
such a proper gent.

Mike Jenkins

Wishful Thinking

The lost royal wanders over, attempts a smile,
asks how to reach the forest, waves his shotgun,
says, *It's mine, you know, all mine.*

I put my finger to my lips as if to ponder routes.
I gaze up to the sky then back at him, and tell him,
*Since we're standing here in Wood Street,
it can't be far away. Just let me think.*

I make him wait while I stop to listen to some
recent colonizers high above our tatty roadside
London limes—so many gulls so far from sea.

I turn to face him, tell him that a steady stroll
along this road will bring him to a busy junction
with a grassy roundabout where once, not all that
long ago, cows black and white would graze
and raise their heads as we walked though.

No longer there, of course, I add. *Too many
cars these days to feel that they'd be safe.*

His Range Rover's still purring by the kerb.
He merely sighs and waits for more, hand
stretched ready and impatiently towards
its open door. I like a sigh so copy his.

These days, I'm so forgetful, I (almost)
apologize. *Can you just remind me
where it is you want to go?*

The forest, he repeats, and can't resist—
It's mine, you know.

Denni Turp

Dogbite

The corgi that bit me
on Hermingdale Road
must have known
that my dad
didn't like the Queen
as it sunk royalist teeth
into my Republican wrist.

One of the things
my dad used to say,
fairly regular,
was that the Royals
wouldn't invite
the likes of us
around for dinner.

He was right,
they never did.

Kenny Knight

Charlie Boi

Charlie Boi lives up Cefn
ewge ouse like a manshun,
local celebritee always on–a telly
bangin on 'bout is lovely trees
an ow ee cares f'r animals.

Some locals treat im like royalty
coz of is MBE an ee gives em
Chris'mas dinner ev'ry year free
in–a village all. 'Ooo tha Charlie,'
they d' say, 'ee's soooo kind!'

Int so generous to is staff mind,
on pittance pay, though there's one guy
local writer name o Gray
follows im round like a corgi,
even speaks Welsh .... ee's on a lead.

President of a wildlife charitee
buh ewsed t be fox-untin on is land
an yew're noh tellin me
is cows an lambs don' end up
as Sundiy roasts with gravy.

Knew this bloke arrested f fishin
up Charlie's estate, gotta big fine.
Even goh is own eraldree
with an oak an a deer—
fee seen one, ee'd reach f is gun!

Mike Jenkins

40

Appointed? Anointed?

They asked me to be monarch.
I said, no way! I'm not that evil.
They said, you get to wear a crown
and be anointed by the arch of cant.
I said, that's a weird kink. Not my bag.
They said, you'll get millions of pounds
and you get to tell the populace
to give to the needy. With your gold crown
next to you. We're not kidding.
I said, I'd have to be a psychopath.
The worst kind. The worst ruler.
They said, we know...
...but you should see what we're lumbered with...

Cathy Bryant

The Great British Buffalo   *

In my 'unicorn kingdom'
all creatures shall be sovereign,
whether feral or domestic,
imaginary or real.
For I am crowned with backward horns
and a fuzzy wig between.

You will enjoy (and fund)
a tax-light, start-up ecosystem.
Beneath the sway of my tail,
beetles will breed high-growth companies
in the magical—and all too often
unattainable—dung.

While I gaze at the vanishing grass
oxpeckers eat my ticks;
may pick fresh wounds to drink the blood.
Unless they pierce my soft belly—
heavy with wealth—I shall not care:
for they have sworn allegiance.

Monarch of the swamp,
ruler of these rising waters,
I might not be the overlord
you had hoped for.
Seventy years is quite some age to loiter,
waiting to be anointed.

Mark Cassidy

* https://www.irishtimes.com/business/2023/04/29/welcome-to-the-unicorn-kingdom-says-sunak-in-fantasy-pitch-to-business/
https://www.youtube.com/watch?v=wICvpM2Kvlg

Insanely Arcane

Before his crown is placed upon his head
His minions wasted no time at all
Mugs with his image wreathed in kingdom flags
Are handed out to all new kids at school,
Get them whilst they're young, print subservience
Upon innocent tabula rasa.
Teach them how important it is to bow,
To curtsey, to scrape, to accept blue blood.
Never to question stolen enclosed land,
Become automata, die in their name,
Maintain royal privilege, play their game,
Swallow old customs hook, line, and sinker,
Don't educate, stifle free thinkers,
Stir god into mix, insanely arcane.

Harry Rogers

Privatize the King

if you aspire to the upper class,
swoon at accents like cut glass
then we have got a marvellous deal for you

only patriots need apply,
ours is not to reason why
just get in quick for this tremendous coup.

It's the investment of a lifetime,
and it's one you must not miss
it's all you've ever dreamed of,
we know you'll all be keen

put your money where your mouth is,
anticipate ka-ching!
show how much you love him,
as we privatize the King!

You've got to admit it makes such sense
to privatize the monarchy
let admirers stump up pounds and pence,
to maintain the Royal Family

remove the Royal drain
upon the ailing public purse
save them all from abolition,
or maybe even worse.

It'll really give you all a stake,
in the family that loves to take
this sell-off really takes the cake,
the best decision you'll ever make

Has there ever been such high romance,
such an eager queue of sycophants
all wetting their proverbial pants,
you know you've got to take the chance

and of course there will be benefits,
if you invest your cash
there'll be lavish invitations,
to the next palatial bash

there'll be titles given out like sweets,
there'll be parties in the streets
an extra spesh investors badge,
from His or Her or perhaps Their Maj

imagine being able
to really truly own
a polo horse, a corgi,
a bit of fancy throne

a piece of fuselage
from the latest Royal plane
a fancy claret carriage
of the exclusive Royal train

own a few square feet of Windsor
adopt a beefeater or two
put your investment funds into
that fabled golden Royal loo

nothing demonstrates your loyalty
commitment to our royalty
like crowdfunding the suppression
of the next awkward indiscretion

royalists in rhapsodies,
fantasies of fame
of gratitude bestowed,
to elevate your family name

a bit of pomp and ceremony,
a flock of heirs and spares
and you can take the credit
with your royal stocks and shares

if it's good enough for water, and good enough for gas
to be sold off to grifters who make profits quite absurd
If we can sell off Royal Mail, and the NHS is up for sale
then it's a perfect time to buy a share of Chuck the Turd

Just a final word of warning
as you gamble on the crown
The value of shares might well go up
but might just as well go down.

Vron McIntyre

* *Based on a post by my late mother Pat McIntyre on her satirical blog.*

Coronation Blues

Bring out the china for Charles.
Bring out bunting made in China.
Bring out prawn rings from Iceland.
Bring out blood crowns from Empire.
Bring out Diana faded on Grandma's mug.
Bring out the other mugs who voted for the blues.

Bring out soldiers from cribs of old cardboard.
Bring out plastic police on minimum wage.
Bring out real police with Austrian guns.
Bring out princes with Austrian blood.
Bring out Phantoms of Rolls Royce.
Bring out killers with clean hands.

Bring out the sell-out laureate.
Write laundered poems without soul.
Edit out views of Grenfell on the Beeb.
Edit out royal letters to the neon paedophile.
Edit out 'racist' from Churchill raised above us.
Edit out traitors with puncturing questions of England.

Zoom in on everything that makes us proud to be British.
Zoom in on Balti houses and Turkish barbers.
Zoom in on immigrant Latin inscriptions.
Zoom into the Abbeys they made.
Zoom into the Kings they made.
Zoom into the lies we chose.

Antony Owen

Waste of Time!, Martin Gollan

Royal Visit to Headingley Stadium

What do you do?

> said the prince to the groundsman

who thought

> What a bloody stupid question,
> given I'm sat on a lawnmower, which
> you've just watched me drive from one
> side of the field to the other

but said

> I'm the resident artist here, and
> I'm making a picture there on the grass,
> that might not seem like anything much,
> but when it's done it should look grand,
> though not from here, you see it's made
> in a way that means it can only be seen
> from space

and the prince said

> It's great to have art in sport,
> how very nice to meet you

but thought

> What a waste of time and money

and the groundsman thought

> the same

Joe Williams

49

Wolves Come Grovelling (Again)   *

Out of the forests of towns & hovelling,
Wolves of poverty, howl out in worship,
Bow to your Wolf-king, wolves come grovelling.

Forget soaring bills & the cost of living
For one weekend, spaff on wolf-fellowship,
Out of the forests of towns & hovelling.

His crowned head, minted on our pound sterling
& postage stamps, shadows our hardship—
Bow to your Wolf-king, wolves come grovelling.

Grab the bank holiday, string out the bunting,
You're Subjects of strung-along citizenship—
Out of the forests of towns & hovelling;

It's all just so much Cat–Rat–&–Lovelling
Of Saxe–Coburg–Gotha & kingship—
Bow to your Wolf-king, wolves come grovelling.

Mark the Coronation by volunteering
Community penance/unpaid stewardship—
Out of the forests of towns & hovelling,
Bow to your Wolf-king, wolves come grovelling.

Alan Morrison

* https://www.youtube.com/watch?v=xWidCJ94lDM&ab_channel=CaparisonPoetry

50

Not Yours to Take

Come down!
Come down!
Red white and blue
In overdose,
As the man in the big hat
Takes his seat
On the undemocratic throne
Of our mass stolen heritage.

They stole
The gold,
The land,
The people.

Took it all,
And now we are expected
To celebrate,
As we suffer poverty
Because mummy's dead
And her son,
Has an ersatz right
To something that was never anyone's
To begin with.

Sam Marshall

Welcome to ....

The Coronation News
The Coronation Weather
The Coronation Cooking
Featuring Coronation Chicken
Followed by ....
The Coronation Clothes Show
Highlighting the golden mantle
Inlaid with slaves' eyeballs
And the Coronation queuing
With Coronation people
Wearing butchers' aprons.

Welcome to ....
The Coronation train
Cancelled, late, delayed
Where you can hear those royals—
      'Mind the gap'
Between their filthy riches
And us lowly serfs—
You'll fall into it
Be run over and mangled.

Welcome to
The Cor.... Cor.... Cor.... Cor....
Release them,
Release those ravens

Mike Jenkins

England in 2022

One of the princely dregs
lies in waiting, (lying in state),
to become a despised King.

Wait in line leech like.
Bide the time in ceremony,
to fill an empty space.

With a 'Prime Monster' elected by a
tiny rump of Tory vermin. Feeling
nothing for the foodbank poor.

Lies! The currency of Capital—too
absorbed to see small nations
clawing free of the Butcher's Apron.

Weather vane warning—
storms to come;
through workplace and community.

Let lightning strike
and thunder roar—
phantoms no more...

Des Mannay

Nah, You're Alright, Martin Gollan

Nah, You're Alright

I'd rather do a highland fling
Or tie my nipples up with string
Impale my buttock on a spring
I'd rather do most anything
Than pledge allegiance to a king

I'd risk the wrath of Merciless Ming
Or face what fierce tornados bring
I'd rather drape myself in bling
Or swallow insects on the wing
Than pledge allegiance to a king

I'd rather fall from a garden swing
Or pierce my lips with a hornet sting
I'd rather choke on a wedding ring
Or live in bogs where crawdads sing
Than pledge allegiance to a king

I'd rather drown in a thermal spring
Or join a protest in Beijing
Go ten rounds in a boxing ring
Or leave a party in full swing
Than pledge allegiance to a king

Or any unelected thing
I'll never bow down to a king

Janine Booth

Corodividednation

by now, of course, you'll know
the way the day panned out

mid-morning, the mood dark
as skies, heavy as policing

abbey filled with the great and good
whose mouths taste of leather

whose souls are spreadsheets
their world an unending transaction

who watch the robe presented
to a rough sleeper curled in a doorway

on Euston Road his filthy sleeping bag
laid upon the monarch's shoulders

the holy oil, brought up the aisle
in a dinghy found on Dover beach

to Canterbury, life-jacketed, sodden,
who drips salt water and the echo of prayers

in Albanian, Dari, Farsi, and homegrown
poverty over the heads of the congregation

the jewelled sword of offering
the bracelets of sincerity and wisdom

pawned for foodbanks in forgotten towns
where bread and tinned goods count for more

than any circus

that Black Power salute
a thing of wonder

nightingale singing in Berkeley Square
the Thames running out to the sea

Steve Pottinger

I Am Nobody's Subject

I am nobody's subject, nor object,
but I am a verb—a doing word,
not passive, but active,
I am vocative,
evocative, provocative,
high-octane, profane, insane, vain,
permissive, not submissive,
unapologetically frenetic,
ecstatic, emphatic, empathic,
over-emotional, often dramatic.

I am nobody's subject, and I object
to bowing down before a throne
and chanting allegiance
to unelected leaders,
My rules are my own,
I need no Rule Britannia,
I dangle no bunting
of red, white and blue.
I shall not chant platitudes
nor speak of gratitude to Royalty
whilst waiting in the food bank queue.

God save us from the King,
God save us from all things
that would seek to convince us
we are anything less than equals
on this small, blue, beautiful planet,
for were we not born to love one another?
And if we are sister and brother,
how can we walk past uncaring
when some have nothing
and those at the top aren't sharing,
and people are staring
at a street man who has no shoes,

whilst another man,
on the Six o'clock News,
is given a crown set with diamonds,
and everyone cheers?
This is everything that is wrong with the world.
I am nobody's subject, nor object,
but a question mark:
how much longer will you tolerate this?

Rebecca Lowe

To Crown It All, Martin Gollan

To Crown It All

As far as the news went, all the wars
in Sudan, Ukraine, Yemen, and anywhere
else were suspended; no one whatsoever
died of Covid; no celebrities did anything
remotely celebretitious; no crimes were
committed, whether violent or otherwise;
there were no major accidents and no
natural disasters; nothing went extinct;
bizarre coincidences failed to coincide.

The glaring shortage of factoids left
the media havering between panic and
a self-destructive blamefest. But someone
had happened on an interminable ceremony
in a minor, post-imperial European nation.
The vultures descended, gorged for hours,
regurgitating regularly for an audience
denied any choice of infotainment.

Next day people went about with a strange
look on their faces, a blend of shame,
bewilderment, and momentary flashes
of relief as they realized that neither they
nor anyone else were ever going to say
one word about the orgy of inanities
from which they were slowly coming round.

Rip Bulkeley

As the New King's Lord Chamberlain Imbibed Free Wine While Sat in His Free Seat

he saw the clown already explaining to the king and his lover
                                                    that the marriage
to his estranged (though not as strange as him) wife (who'd been
                                                    in her own tryst)
had been crushed by an overturned carriage—so you now
                                                    need only one divorce.
After an in-front-of-tabs spot-lit mimed wedding, in loud scene
                                                    after loud scene
the king's two sons called each other out over fancy dress,
                                                    rivalries, privileges,
taking local or foreign wives, until one got banished
                                                    before the last act began
where, after a trumpet fanfare, the sovereign sat upstage
                                                    as robed nobles processed,
knelt to pledge allegiance before the clown turned, walked downstage
                                                    —opened his arms,
asked the audience if they'd swear loyalty instead. Sudden darkness.
                                                    Stuttering applause.
Now in a no longer full theatre the Lord Chamberlain sits
                                                    on its make-believe throne
as the writer explains, It's fiction: a made-up king, country, clown.
                                                    So a play can say
everything we all know (dramatic pause)—or, as with Lear,
                                                    its end might change?
Again, the wine jug's tipped (he'd poured and sipped sack
                                                    all through the play)
while he hears how this plot got stirred like suet, cinnamon, mace,
                                                    in mincemeat pies;
is reminded he's seen plays—tragedies with dysfunctional rulers,
                                                    wives, sons, clowns;
with adulteries, sudden deaths, sibling rivalries—but the list
                                                    omits drunkenness!
Because, as the night's crowd soberly walks home, talking over
                                                    what's been staged,

62

the jug's empty. Writer and clown watch the man stand, all three
                                        goblets brim full—
their two unseen hands' fingers crossed behind doublet and hose
                                        when the jug falls
as the one with the power to recommend the next day's beheadings
                                        sways,
steadies himself, slurs *All that's left is the toast* (loud belch)
                                        to The King.

Bob Cooper

Unentitled

Now when the black-sleeved muffled-down drum is silent
and all the shrouded union flags lowered from their jacks
when the scarlet and gold soldiers no longer mark time
to drill ground orders and another brass band's beat.

When the right-eyed queen lies in her crypt underground
the splinter still works its way out of the thin-lined wound
and still the fragments in the wound ooze and seep
and they still tell us in their rituals we do not exist.

Wiping it in our faces again.

Funeral, wedding, coronation,
it doesn't matter what they call it,
call it what they will,
they're wiping it in our faces again.

Demanding subservience,
sick-making obedience,
bending the knee, bowing the head,
a curtsy one to three.

Demanding we show respect—
But must we lower ourselves
in the face of their entitlement,
in the face of their arrogance?

Why don't we turn our backs,
look the other way, anywhere away,
from this bunch of inbred thieves.
Deny them the oxygen of publicity,
after all that's what you do with terrorists,
colonialists will even rob the graves,
of the people whose lands they destroy.

Rob Cullen

64

Pledge of Allegiance

I pledge allegiance to my sons
to witty jokes and dreadful puns
I pledge allegiance to Aussie soaps
to chasing all my dreams and hopes
I pledge my allegiance to the Borough boys
to Lewes FC, to making noise
I pledge allegiance to classic scooters
I pledge to battle persecutors
to fight injustice till it's gone
I pledge to keep on keeping on

I pledge myself to ranting verse
For good, for better and for worse

I pledge allegiance to The Force
and to the Jedi Code of course
Allegiance to the Rebel Alliance
Insurgency and bold defiance
I pledge myself to rise and shine
to never cross a picket line
I pledge allegiance to the working class
to never let injustice pass
I pledge allegiance to the fight
I pledge myself to human rights
I pledge my allegiance to democracy
and never to autocracy
I pledge my allegiance to scotch and tonic
but never ever to a monarch

Janine Booth

65

The Crowning Glory

It's Coronation Chicken time in Coronation Street.
Everyone is down at The Crown.
The flags are out and flying, tweeters strain to tweet,
Security cams are planted everywhere in town.
It will be a knees-up, a proper royal fling,
With loyal oaths in chorus to welcome in the King.

Oh Britain, land of Monarchs, all panoply and pomp,
The island may be sinking but we float.
Although we're mostly paupers, the nation's set to romp
While clinging to the sides of the boat.
It may be just a knees-up with shoelaces of string
But we will kick our heels up in honour of the King.

Every royal has his place, peers will find their niche,
The spectacle's designed to overwhelm.
Some will feast on food-banks, some on royal quiche,
There's feasting in the gutters of the realm.
Everything is ready now, time to don the bling.
Blow up the balloons, young man, pop one for the King.

We're well equipped with princes in case we need a spare,
Our substitutes are warmed up on the bench,
With extra teams of royals, should we require an heir,
Plus junior ranks lined up in the trench.
Before the match the royal team will stand round in a ring.
The ref checks with the linesmen. Blows. It's kick-off for the King.

George Szirtes

66

Cost of Living

It hangs dead, under the lychgate
hidden in the shadow
of the poisonous yew.

In a forgotten churchyard
where Spanish Bluebells
and Snowbells grow.

It is there outside the playgroups
the quite care homes, a moment
none of them will remember tomorrow.

It lingers, like discarded food packaging.
This grandeur makes some feel secure,
while their neighbours go hungry next door.

Patrick Druggan

Not My King, Mike Dicks

One of Us

1—Plural

I live in a country that is not mine and proud to spend millions pumping up a Trident of pomp, quiche and stirring music. The Liverpool fans who booed the national anthem are lucky: in the days when subjects wore the king in their wallets, royalty didn't always take kindly to a distaste for the monarchy.

It was a triumph, a milestone between Dublin and London: The Irish Delegation set precedent by showing respect to Britain. Alas, VIP Matt didn't get the memo. He kept his phone on and boyfriend Leo was filmed picking his nose, just as the queen consort touched the Sceptre and Rod! Red faces all around! What a symbolic gesture for Ireland!

2—Singular

Surrounded by a wet Union and inflatable crowns, the Upholder of the Protestant Faith in Divine Right mutters as he goes past in his gold carriage (fitted with electric windows)

> *Yes, I am*
> *we can never be*
> *on time*
> *there is always*
> *something*
> *this is so boring*

Oh, the very heavy lifting of that crown! Ah, but he doesn't have to smell us, ah, he doesn't have to feel our sweat, and it's all on us.

3—Protest

Police, police, here we come. Acting on intelligence, they arrested fifty-two people for possession of strings and luggage straps. The straps will be used for a locking-in protest, create havoc and panic, in a vile plot to spook kings and horses. That's the drama of a terrorist swoop.

Protest, arrest, a farcical case, unrest. How do you ensure the situation doesn't escalate? We were just there to avoid the coronation, miles away, after tracking the Croydon Cat Killer. It was a day of intense learning for everyone. They were all talking at once: *You're under arrest.* Why? *Do not sip your coffee, it could be poisoned or something.* I asked for a solicitor and was served a vegan all-day breakfast instead, which was literally ALL beans. I want my phone and watch back, says Matt.

The police have declined to comment.

Mélisande Fitzsimons

Coronation Day

I wake from anxious dreams,
roll out of bed. Looking from the window,
I see that it is not raining.
A fine day for it, after all.

I can hear the rumble of tumbrel wheels
in the yard outside, and further on
the crowds are cheering. Who they cheer for,
I do not know. My head is aching.

I still maintain that I was not bad.
Born to the wrong place, wrong time,
an ill-starred name.

It is hard to know the etiquette
for such occasions.
Should one wear a tie?

Philip Kane

Old Important Bloke

Coronation chicken and blueberry juice.
Orange ticketed, further reduced!
Old bloke on TV in some golden robes,
Similar clothes to Supreme Leader Snoke.
Crown on swede, massive lobes!
Crowds applaud the lavish show.
Can't watch for long, leccy is gonna go.
Poverty continues, but he'll never know.
Soldiers salute, horsemen in the saddle,
Loyal and astute, ready for anyone's battle,
A national commute, herds of human cattle.
'Oh wonderful, I'm going to cry',
The old ladies prattle.
Like hordes of rats, hearing a flute!
Scampering down the most regal of routes.
Awaiting the Royal Artillery's boom!
Red Arrows burn fuel for a million rooms.
Nicholas Witchell, stroking his nipples.
Anarchists show respect!
Please? Just a little?
The whole occasion is one big fiddle!
Prince Andrew lurking, hiding in the middle.
Civilians camped in rapturous streets.
Oblivious cheers on damp concrete.
All in unity, or so said the Police.
Clowns to the South, beasts to the East.
Royalists shed momentous tears.
The greatest spectacle in 70 years!
Brittania's minions, doing it properly.
Inherited billions, plus the Queen's Property
We all pass Go, but they play Monopoly.
All hail the latest state of Monarchy!
Sworn to be a servant, to us lucky slaves.
So I guess we'll be grateful,
Every fucking day!

Gareth Twamley

Local News

Where I live in Kilburn, London, is a street
With a couple of hundred houses either side,
Tall and Victorian, a few more modern,
Each divided into three or four apartments,
So that's a lot of windows
And yet only one decked out for the Coronation,
Home to an elderly couple, who I know
Have serious mental health issues, depression
The woman in particular, often found wandering
In slippers and her dressing gown,
God Save the King and Queen Camilla
They've put Union flags
In their window box
And closed the curtains
Against intrusion
I could be cruel but it feels unnecessary

Steven Taylor

Before, Martin Gollan

Before

Before crowds gathered to see and be seen
Before their Jac yr Undeb hats, flags, clothing
Before the military march and fly-past
Before the golden carriage boasting wealth
Before they even had time to think
Before they could raise their voices
Before their placards were lifted high
Before they could settle, organize
Before vicious royalists could yell insults
Before TV crews could ignore them
Before the Great Context had begun
Before he'd been anointed by a Protestant god
Before bells in posh parishes were rung
Before Cymru's empty chairs for the screening
Before anyone could chant 'Not our king!'
They were arrested, taken.

Mike Jenkins

* Jac yr Undeb = Union Jack

Coronation Song of the One Percent

Thousands were making the precarious climb
up the front of the palace which appeared
three times the normal height,
to pay their respects
to the royals; they were numberless
salmon that had leapt the waterfalls
with their dying praise.
You would think it was innate.
There was television coverage.
With the sound off
the selection of shots
was a lesson in deference
to the celebs and toffs.
They were intimate and safe
to us. How remote
the relief of rage.
How we were schooled
in vacuous reverence:
it was something we did well,
it made us feel better
though tomorrow
we'd be worse off,
hung over, with for some
a bitter aftertaste,
a lurking sense
of being fleeced.
It was obvious who was to blame
once we'd tucked away the ambulances
and the bunting for the next time:
it was that something for nothing
generation. How we yearned
for a smaller state
for the people just out of vision,
and welfare reform
for the malingerers we knew about

from the depth of our prompted being.
The wealth of the One Percent
grew bloated, out of proportion
as with water on the brain:
we share the cranial compression.
We missed the industrious
collusion offscreen.
We pay tribute to them,
the subliminal movers and shakers
who are cleverer than us,
who minimize the corporation tax
with their quick fingers
and their soporific tricks.
It's decades now,
and the long-tailed wisp
of the stink of hocus-pocus
lingers on over us

Steve Griffiths

I Pledge My Allegiance

I pledge my allegiance
To the source from whence I came
To the one divine creator
To that which has no name
To the power in and of me,
That rules all I touch and see
It never has to prove itself
Because I know it cares for me.

I pledge my allegiance
Not to a gilded throne,
Or to crowns and jewels historic,
Or to ceremonial stone
But to souls of pure intention
To those born of the light
And, standing at my side, unhindered
Still fight for what is right.

I pledge my allegiance
To those who guide my hand
Unseen but ever-present
They are the rulers of this land
This land and every other
The planets, moons and stars
Who guide the fates of mortal kings
Who heal my wounds and scars
Who protect me from the darkness,
And light the path ahead
Who reward me with experience,
And will raise me from the dead
I pledge my allegiance
To the one true consciousness
The one you've all forgotten
The one who loves me best.

I pledge my allegiance
With every earthly breath
To the cradle of creation
My home, come mortal death
Immortal I become then
And I will join with thee
And next you pledge allegiance
That pledge you'll make to me.

Andrew Greenhalgh

Headpieces

Not one but two, before and after anointment.
Symbols of inheritance each with its own lineage.

St Edward's traced to an early heritage, a dynastic start.
Imperial as a mark of what is owned; gifted or bought.

Each of them carefully monitored around the clock.
Each of them admired in a guarded display cabinet.

Reset over the years, modest changes to alignment,
gems pronged out, cleaned, a tweak or two in position.

The velvet restored, silk resewn, weasel fur defleaed
for each head they surmount on noble occasions.

Know where each jargoon and blood carbuncle was mined,
which firm sliced each facet of the Cullinan's reflection.

Our monarch crowned as a vainglorious tourist attraction,
the dazzle of stones for proles to capture on their phones.

State owned and their uses infinitely thought through.
Sold and broken, how many food banks could be stocked?

Sue Spiers

Vanishing Point

Search for point where aristocrats vanish,
There is a hopeful perspective somewhere.
We can draw conclusions in our own way
If we take time, look long and hard enough.
Everything we do benefits greatly
From investigation and reflection.
Surrounded by baubles, bishops and bunk,
Overwhelmed with fanfares and stately junk,
Weighed down with Crown affixed to royal bonce,
Trapped, unable to cast a look askance,
One can but wonder what he really feels,
Now that everyone curtseys and kneels.
His eyes watched whilst minions didst anoint,
Perhaps he's seen his own vanishing point.

Harry Rogers

Invite, Martin Gollan

Invite

Blocking the entrance to the Abbey
is an African elephant and her calf.
She doesn't seem to care
that the king and queen can't get in
but then neither do the mink or the stoats
or the goats munching away on prayer books
or the ostriches keeping very still
or the wobbly lambs just finding their feet
or the cows sitting placid and wise in the aisle.
No one seems to know what to do
but even if they could find a way in
they wouldn't be able to hear the archbishop
over the chatter and screech of the birds above the altar
and anyway all the seats have already been taken
by miners—still caked in dust and sweat
but taking deep breaths of the fresh, clean air,
broken bones healed and red eyes wide in disbelief.

Ian Harker

Crown & Sceptre, Friday 9th September, 4.15pm

and Niall is telling the barmaid he's going to ring the lawyer he
is he is he's going to ring the lawyer as she nods and smiles
nods and smiles and pours because it's doing his head in it's
doing his bastard head in and yeah go on he'd like another
Bud and he prowls like a tiger in a backwater pub where all
the screens are set to sports channels but there are
no sports to show

and Shane and Mark pop in for just a quick one to wash
the Junction 10 dust from the back of their throats and
the quick one will be four or five at least as Shane and Mark
and the barmaid all know and she smiles and pours and
smiles and smiles and pours and they've a regular wage
and hi–vis, you can see them both from space and all
the screens are set to horse racing
but there's no horse race

and the lads who drank at The Eagle until The Eagle
closed are at the table in the corner so they can see
who comes and goes the barmaid pours their lager
pours their lager pours their lager and they offer her
a grin and the sports channels say no football and
yes this means that this week you can't lose
it doesn't mean you ever win

and they're all bucket hats and swagger and they're ready
to take flight and one of them's a mouth that's guaranteed
to lead his fists into a fight and the barmaid keeps an eye
on them and they think she could be flirting but she's
smiling pouring nodding and she thinks she's almost certain
that laughter's not offensive kicking a ball is nothing wrong
and channels made for sport should have some sport on

and the men who last had jobs when there were factories
in this town who have a Friday evening pint as if the work
was still around and the plasterers and painters and the
plumbers and the drivers and the blokes who have a market
stall the shift workers and skivers are all in here for the craic
a pint perhaps who knows a short and the barmaid smiles and
nods and smiles and nods and smiles and nods and pours
in this backwater pub on a Friday where sports channels
don't show sport

Steve Pottinger

Succession Fanning, Martin Gollan

Succession Fanning

Republicanism is so yesterday darling,
deep fawn is the new black.
Reds, whites and blues
are the back-in-vogue hues,
we've cut out guides to keep you on track.

It's Carry On As You Were Luvvie,
Kiss-me-quick hats and union flags.
Donald McGill postcards flutter supple
as we all suck up to a rich old couple,
while the broke sleep out on carrier bags.

Nationalism is so the thing sweetie,
don your blazers and boaters.
Don't think about recession,
just watch the succession
of the oh-so-English Saxe–Coburg–Gothas.

Harry Gallagher

Chaos Without Care

The order of today
Is chaos without care,
Take a good look around,
There's bodies everywhere.
Trot off around our world,
Spread bullets, bombs and fear,
Ramp up faux pageantry,
Crown a billionaire.
Roll out old golden coach
As horse guards bob along,
Affirm those empire days,
Sing out loud that tired song,
Nothing less anthemic,
Keep weakest below strong,
Westminster Abbey bells,
Ding dong, ding dong, ding dong.
I still recall last time,
In nineteen fifty three,
That jelly and blancmange,
Black and white TV screen,
Same old same old same old,
Banner flags on our streets,
Media orgasmic,
Plus Richard Dimbleby.
Back then we all had hope,
We'd not long won the war,
Parents beat those Nazis,
They knew what they'd fought for.
Seventy years later
Many are not too sure,
Prejudice is rampant,
They've locked that Brexit door.
This time round I'll not watch
Arcane brainwash TV,
No pomp nor circumstance

Nor glitter will tempt me.
I'll be onstage with band
At Picklesfest for free,
Dance in our own mudbath,
In twenty twenty three.

Harry Rogers

Long to Rain O'er Us, Mike Dicks

End of

A sea of Union Jack umbrellas
& see-through ponchos—
Royalists saturated in Coronation rain
rain-pattered pageantry
rain rain for the brand new reign

Metropolitan patters on yellow placards
packed up into the back of a police van
along with several republican protestors
including Republic's urbane CEO
before they had a chance to unpack them,
along with their megaphones—
all confiscated in the cause of policing
democratic protest—
the demonstrators detained for sixteen
hours without explanation

<u>Journalist:</u> *Why are people being arrested*
for protesting in a democracy?
<u>Policeman:</u> *I'm not going to get into*
a conversation about that,
they are under arrest, end of.

Let that be an advertisement
while the world is watching the Coronation—
in Britain peaceful protest is now
suppressed even when it's not disruptive
as peaceful protestors are arrested
before they've had the chance to protest

This signals the end of peaceful protest
being tolerated in Britain.
End of.

Alan Morrison

Man on Chair Clicks Open Pen

it's not the King
being wheeled along in his inglorious refinery
down the Mall
it's not the tax dodging
selling Duchy of Cornwall to Waitrose
on the back of inheritance and land grab
with nothing offered to the Chancellor
as he takes the percents each month
from our hard earned pounds
it's not the castles and the palaces
the soft boiled eggs
brought to him every morning
by a butler in grey tails
only to later hear
about his suffering
it's not even the Crown Jewels
stolen from another country
or the passive aggressive use of the media
to awaken us
to their ilk's pain
it's not any of that—
these things will always happen
in an on-going class war
it's the poet
raised from working-class stock
who hit it with Kid
now using a fictitious woman
travelling down from the North
to try and convince us
to celebrate it
that's what it is for me
that's what's got me today
the poet

Martin Hayes

Carolus Windsor *

Carolus Windsor got sick of his wife,
Hee-haw sick of his wife;
He took him another to sweeten his life,
Hee-haw sweeten his life.

His stubborn old mother would never concur,
Hee-haw never concur;
But Carolus couldn't leave things as they were,
Hee-haw things as they were.

So Carolus gave her a bit of a smack,
Hee-haw bit of a smack,
And his mother fell flippity flat on her back,
Hee-haw flat on her back.

The mobile and charger lie there on the shelf,
Hee-haw there on the shelf;
If you want any more you can tweet it yourself,
Hee-haw tweet it yourself.

Rip Bulkeley

* To hear Benjamin Britten's setting of the traditional 'Oliver Cromwell' rhyme,
sung by Peter Pears, go here: https://www.youtube.com/watch?v=VdMJUVhsVnY

About the editor

Rip Bulkeley is a more or less retired political activist, peace researcher and historian of the Cold War, the earth sciences, and Antarctica. He has been trying to write better poetry for 68 years. His début as an organizer was the 1960 Adelaide students' 'Prosh' (rag day), and as a protester, the 1962 Aldermaston March. He founded Oxford's thriving Back Room Poets in 1999, and published *War Times* with Ripostes in 2003. He speaks 5½ languages, has lived in four countries, and edited seven anthologies including this one. Three of the others were *Poems for Grenfell Tower* (Onslaught, 2018), *Rebel Talk* (Extinction Rebellion Oxford, 2021), and *A Fish Rots From the Head* (Culture Matters, 2022).

About the poets

Alan Morrison is the author of eleven volumes of poetry, his most recent, *Wolves Come Grovelling*, is a collection of republican poems. His poem 'Shelleyan Threnody' was highly commended in the Shelley 200 Festival (Horsham) Poetry Competition 2022.

Andrew Greenhalgh is a creative marketing consultant by day, writing ad copy for clients. By night he's a winner of the British song writing contest, and currently working on his first sci-fi novel.

Anne Babbs is a working-class poet from the Black Country. She reads at open mic events and has had work published in the *New Voices* anthology published by Offa's Press.

Antony Owen has a forthcoming *New & Selected* book out in summer 2024 from Broken Sleep Books.

Bob Cooper now lives on the Wirral. In the 1990s he won five pamphlet competitions in six years. His third full collection, *Listening, listening*, is forthcoming from Naked Eye.

Cathy Bryant is a multi-award-winning, disabled bisexual writer whose books include *Look at All the Women* (Mother's Milk) and *Erratics* (Arachne). Think 'Carol Ann Duffy meets Spike Milligan'.

Chris Norris is a poet, philosopher, member of Cor Cochion Caerdydd (Cardiff Reds Choir), and lives in Swansea.

Deborah Cox-Walker was born in New York but educated in England, where she developed a love of English literature. She is currently organizing her first poetry collection. Her website is DeborahCox.co.uk.

Denni Turp is a Welsh-speaking working-class Cockney, a green socialist republican, a dog adopter, and Vice-Chair of Disability Arts Cymru, with poems published in poetry magazines, anthologies and webzines.

Des Mannay is a disabled, Welsh writer of colour. Collection *Sod 'em—and tomorrow* (Waterloo Press, 2020). Co-editor *The Angry Manifesto* journal. Prizewinner in four competitions, shortlisted in seven, in 39 anthologies. Judge in *Valiant Scribe* competition (USA).

Ed Tapper is a Plymouth poet and artist. He published his first collection of poems *Easy Peelers* last year; his second, *A Pocket for the Fist of Empire*, will appear in 2024.

Edward Mackinnon has worked as a translator in the Netherlands and France. Four collections of his poetry have been published by Shoestring Press.

Fin Hall is from New Pitsligo, Scotland. He has work in print in over 40 different publications and about 10 online including two solo collections. He is also a filmmaker and producer.

Gareth Twamley is an actor, poet and spoken word practitioner from South Wales. His work certainly has a Punk edge. Previously he created Cardiff events 'Lyrical Miracles' and 'Word Asylum'.

George Cruikshank (1792-1878) was the leading political caricaturist and illustrator in nineteenth-century England, taking over that role from his equally famous predecessor James Gillray.

George Szirtes is a Hungarian-born poet and translator, author of many books, and winner of the T.S. Eliot Prize 2004.

Harry Gallagher lives in Cullercoats village in Tyneside where he writes poetry. Despite this, the locals remain remarkably tolerant. He is widely published, with several books to his name.

Harry Rogers is a writer at 'retired disgracefully' in the Teifi Valley, West Wales. Currently member of Red Poets of Wales, and lead singer of local rock band Scene Red.

Heather Booker has been writing for decades. Poetry and activism—as socialist, trade-unionist, climate activist and anti-racist—helps to keep her from despair and from throwing things at the telly.

Ian Harker is co-founder of Strix magazine and an organiser of Leeds Lit Fest. His pamphlet *A-Z of Superstitions* is coming through Yaffle in July 2023.

Jackie Biggs has three collections of poetry published. Her fourth will address issues around the climate crisis. She performs her work at events all over west Wales where she lives.

Janine Booth is a Marxist motormouth who tours the UK and beyond, ranting, rhyming and revolting. Her work features in many anthologies, journals and her own books, the latest being *Amplify*.

Jim Jepps is a poet, book seller and flaneur. He's the author of *Anarchism for Dogs* as well as more serious pieces. He comes from Essex but lives in Sheffield.

Joe Williams is a writer from Leeds. His latest book is *The Taking Part* (Maytree Press), a pamphlet of poems on the theme of sport and games.

Johnny Giles is an autistic poet based in Cardiff. His debut pamphlet *Chalk Outlines* (Blackheath Books) was published in 2014. He is currently living in temporary accommodation thanks to Thatcherism.

Kenny Knight has published three collections of poetry with Shearsman Books, the latest being *Love Letter to an Imaginary Girlfriend*. He lives in Plymouth and coedits *Clutter*, the CrossCountry Writers' Journal.

Liz McPherson has been horse-riding in Mongolia and motorcycling in Morocco but tends to stick to poetry now, which is not necessarily a safer pursuit but definitely a less sandy one.

Mark Cassidy is a retired radiographer from Birmingham via the Isle of Wight, and now living in Bury St Edmunds. He writes in the gaps between family, birdwatching, and Oxfam books.

Martin Gollan has worked variously as a community worker, painter, illustrator, printmaker, fervent anti-royalist, Labour Party member / exasperated socialist. See more examples of illustration and printmaking at drawing-ink.com

Martin Hayes has worked in the courier industry for over 30 years. He is the author of seven collections of poetry, which he writes because it makes him feel better than when he doesn't.

Mélisande Fitzsimons has had three collections published in Britain. The latest, *The Only Country in the World* is just out from Aquifer. She writes in both French and English and loves it.

Merryn Williams was the founding editor of *The Interpreter's House* magazine. Her latest poetry collection is *After Hastings* (Shoestring Press), and she edited *Poems for the Year 2020: Eighty Poets on the Pandemic.*

Mike Dicks and his dog Scrabble published two books of his 'Trumpton' parodies of British politics in 2017, and he followed that as 'Michael Mayor' with a third on Donald Trump.

Mike Jenkins is a former comp teacher living in Merthyr Tydfil. Forthcoming: *Igh Sheriff o Merthyr* (Carreg Gwalch), poems in Merthyr dialect, and *Yer Ower Voices!* (Culture Matters), the first ever anthology of dialect poetry from Cymru, in Welsh and English.

Patrick Druggan is a Scot from the East End of Glasgow. He got a free education from the people of this country. He is a scientist, designing diagnostic tests for cancer.

Percy Bysshe Shelley (1792-1822) was a towering figure of the Romantic movement. His other response to Peterloo was *The Masque of Anarchy*, which ends with the stirring declaration 'Ye are many—they are few!'

Phil Knight is a poet and political activist from Neath, South Wales. He has been published in *Red Poets, Atlantic Review, Planet, Poetry Wales*, and elsewhere. In 2015 Red Poets published his collection *You Are Welcome To Wales*.

Philip Kane is published across Europe, the Middle East and the USA; his books include *Unauthorised Person* and *Dramatis Personae*. A member of Anti -capitalist Resistance and the London Surrealist Group.

Rebecca Lowe is a poet, singer, musician and activist from Swansea, Wales. Her latest collection *Our Father Eclipse* is published by Culture Matters.

Rob Cullen lives in South Wales. He is an artist, poet, writer, environmentalist, gardener. Rob walks a lot in the hills and mountains around his home.

Sam Marshall is a former copywriter, author and poet from the UK. He has been writing for five years and enjoys the works of Bukowski, Burroughs and Ginsberg.

Steve Griffiths worked as a researcher, policymaker and campaigner on social and health inequality. His poetry from seven previous collections is gathered in *Weathereye: Selected Poems* (2019). His website is www.stevegriffithspoet.com

Steve Pottinger's work regularly appears online in Culture Matters and the *Morning Star*. His sixth volume of poems, *thirty-one small acts of love and resistance*, is out now.

Steven Taylor is a writer, widely published. Born and raised in Hyde, near Manchester. Currently living in Kilburn, north London.

Stuart Paterson is ex-BBC Scotland Poet-in-Residence, and author of several collections in English and his first language Scots, the latest being *Wheen: New and Collected Poems* from the Ulster Scots Community Network.

Sue Spiers lives in Hampshire and works with Winchester Poetry Festival. Her work is widely published in print and on-line. Sue tweets @spiropoetry.

Vron McIntyre is a queer, disabled poet from Nottingham, who runs the Facebook group Poetry+ Events Online. Their debut pamphlet *Random Trail* was published by Big White Shed in 2021.

BV - #0045 - 100723 - C7 - 210/148/5 - PB - 9781912710621 - Matt Lamination